WHAT PEOPLE ARE SAYING ABOUT
BALANCED CHURCH

I have had the privilege and the joy of knowing Dave Deerman since he arrived in Nashville a number of years ago. I have watched him climb the challenging mountains of ministry and trek his way through the lowest of valleys. He has the two greatest qualities I believe every pastor needs: the inner grit to keep going when times are tough and the humility to always be willing to learn from others. Grit and humility can be taught but very few people catch it. He not only led one of Nashville's mega-churches for a season but came alongside me at Cornerstone Church in Nashville as our Executive Pastor, managing strategic projects, seventeen staff-pastors and their departments, and a congregation of thousands. When the opportunity came, he pioneered one of our campuses in Bowling Green, Kentucky and transformed it into a sovereign church and gracefully installed next pastor. It is growing exponentially today. His insight into church growth, church management, and the paradigm shifts needed to create growth in churches of any size come from education, experience, and passion to keep churches going strong. There are few people I would call pastor, leader, and counselor, and more than anything else—friend. Dave is one of them. I trust him, recommend him, and urge you to let him help your church level up!

—Maury Davis
Maury Davis Ministries
Former Lead Pastor at Cornerstone Church Nashville
Coach, Consultant, Mentor

If you have a God-sized vision and are a forward-thinking leader, do you need someone who can help you implement a workable plan to actually get you there? If so, Dave Deerman is your man. For the past thirty years, I have observed God's gifting of his administrative mind to organize and lead ministries into seasons of exponential growth.

—Terry G. Bailey
District Superintendent
Tennessee Assemblies of God Ministry Network

Dave Deerman is an incredible life coach who holds unique skills to move individuals toward their desired place of destiny. His warm, welcoming, and dynamic personality are special tools he has put to great use to take small things and make them great! He will inspire, motivate, and encourage you to believe and reach for greater things in your personal and professional life. The inspiration of this incredible man I'm blessed to call "friend" will take you to new levels with *Balanced Church*!

—Dr. Chris Bowen
DrChrisBowen@gmail.com
Dream Releaser Coaching Executive Director

Jesus the administrator and organizer? Indeed! Examples? Sending His disciples two by two, sending them as advance teams to His projected itinerary, instructing the disciples how to conduct themselves, seating the 5,000 in specific groupings to distribute food more efficiently, working closely with His Executive Team of three, giving His strategic plan for scaling and sustaining the Church prior to His ascension . . . and many more. Yes, every ministry leader has to be both spiritual leader and administrator. Like the two wings of an airplane—they're both necessary. My friend Dave Deerman unpacks that concept with great experience and encouragement. What a gift to every ministry leader!

—Sam Chand
A Friend of Dave Deerman

As a young pastor in rural America with no ministry training or experience, I was utterly overwhelmed during my first year. Then, I noticed a church experiencing huge growth because of new conversions (lost people being saved) in the county next to mine. I was inspired. I deeply desired for my church to have that same impact. So, I reached out to Pastor Dave Deerman and asked for help. That phone call started a memorable journey for me and my church. I'll forever appreciate Pastor Dave for speaking with me and sharing what seemed to be the "trade secrets"—things that I had never heard before! Through his wisdom and knowledge, I learned how to create guest flow, follow up with guests, implement administration, make the right hiring decisions, and so on. My small country church of sixty eventually became a large one with several sites and an average of 2,000 people on the weekend. I'll always be grateful for Pastor Dave's lessons and friendship.

—Josh Hannah
President and Founder of Compassion Church Network
President and Founder of Hope Center Ministries

Dave is a top-tier thinker with an easy-going style of communication and leadership that enables openness, sustainable business relationships, and next-level growth. Dave builds upon truth to help you thrive in this current culture of uncertainty in leadership.

—Terry Allen
Founder and President
MVP Leader Group
Honoring, Encouraging, and Connecting Leaders

BALANCED CHURCH

ORGANIZING THE CHAOS LEADERS CREATE

DAVE DEERMAN

ARROWS & STONES

Copyright © 2023 by Dave Deerman

Published by Arrows & Stones

All rights reserved. No portion of this book may be reproduced, stored in a retrieval system, or transmitted in any form or by any means—electronic, mechanical, photocopy, recording, scanning, or other—except for brief quotations in critical reviews or articles, without prior written permission of the author.

Scripture quotations marked NKJV are taken from the New King James Version®. Copyright © 1982 by Thomas Nelson. Used by permission. All rights reserved. | The ESV® Bible (The Holy Bible, English Standard Version®). ESV® Text Edition: 2016. Copyright © 2001 by Crossway, a publishing ministry of Good News Publishers. The ESV® text has been reproduced in cooperation with and by permission of Good News Publishers. Unauthorized reproduction of this publication is prohibited. All rights reserved..

For foreign and subsidiary rights, contact the author.

Cover design by Sara Young
Cover photo by Crystal Rodriguez Photography

ISBN: 978-1-959095-55-2   1 2 3 4 5 6 7 8 9 10

Printed in the United States of America

I want to dedicate this book to the woman who, without her encouragement, sacrifice, and love this project of my life's work would have not happened . . . my wife, Christy Deerman. Thank you, Christy, for all your love and sacrifice that helped believe this dream could happen. This project wouldn't be happening if it weren't for you. I love you with all my heart!

CONTENTS

PREFACE xi
ACKNOWLEDGEMENTS xiii
INTRODUCTION 15
WHAT IS A BALANCED CHURCH? 17
MODULE 1 - ASSESSMENTS 19
   1.1 Assessing The Pastor 20
      1.1.1 Leadership Hints 20
      1.1.2 Pastor's Profile 21
   1.2 Assessing Your Staff 22
      1.2.1 Staff Profile 22
   1.3 Assessing Your Church 23
      1.3.1 Each Church is Different 23
      1.3.2 When a Church Grows 24
      1.3.3 Ministry Standing 25
         1.3.3a Where Does Your Ministry Stand? Part 1 25
         1.3.3b Where Does Your Ministry Stand? Part 2 26
         1.3.3c Where Does Your Ministry Stand? Part 3 27
      1.3.4 Church Illness 28
         1.3.4a Signs of Illness Part 1 28
         1.3.4b Signs of Illness Part 2 29
      1.3.5 Church Health 30
         1.3.5a Signs of Health Part 1 30
         1.3.5b Signs of Health Part 2 31
      1.3.6 Church's Profile 32
MODULE 2 - ALL IMPORTANT COMPONENTS FOR GROWTH 33
   2.1 Leadership 34
      2.1.1a Steps to Influence 34
      2.1.1b Steps to Influence Insights 35
      2.1.2 The Big Picture 36
      2.1.3 Vision For Growth 37
         2.1.3a A Clearly Focused Vision 37
         2.1.3b Syndromes That Limit Your Vision 38
         2.1.3c Selling The Vision 39
      2.1.4 Clearly Established Goals 40
      2.1.5 A Clearly Effective Strategy 41
   2.2 Volunteerism 42
      2.2.1 Biblical Background 42
      2.2.2 The Volunteer Principle 43
      2.2.3 The Pareto Principle 80-20 44
      2.2.4 Passion 45
      2.2.5 Volunteer Profile 46

    2.2.6 Generational Differences Balanced Church................................47
2.3 Evangelism 49
    2.3.1 The Evangelism Principle 49
    2.3.2 "Reaching the Unchurched in The 2000's"..............................50
    2.3.3 Increasing Visitor Flow: Making Your List.............................51
    2.3.4 Inviting 52
        2.3.4a What Visitors See 52
        2.3.4b Visitor's Welcome Center 53
    2.3.5 "Make Your List" Strategies 54
2.4 Assimilation 55
    2.4.1 Assimilation Process...55
    2.4.2 Growth Track...56
2.5 Worship..57
    2.5.1 Transitional Mindsets..57
    2.5.2 Positive, Uplifting Worship...58
    2.5.3 Ideas For Meaningful Worship 59
2.6 Stewardship..60
    2.6.1 The Finance Principle 60
2.7 Pastoral Care 61
2.8 Discipleship 62
2.9 Fellowship...63

MODULE 3 - APPLICATION YEAR CALENDAR 65
MODULE 4 - ACQUIRED DISCIPLINES 79
    4.1 Staff And Staffing Relationships Disciplines................................80
    4.1a Discipline 1: Hiring Staff..80
    4.1b Discipline 1 (Cont.): Hiring Staff.......................................81
    4.1c Discipline 2: Conflict Management 82
MODULE 5 - CONTINUED ACCOUNTABILITY RELATIONSHIP 83
APPENDIX 1 - ANSWER SHEETS 85
    A1.1.1 Leadership Hints 86
    A1.3.1 Each Church Is Different 87
    A1.3.2 When A Church Grows 88
    A1.3.3c Where Does Your Ministry Stand?..................................89
    A1.3.4a Signs Of Illness Part 1 90
    A1.3.4b Signs Of Illness Part 2 91
    A1.3.5a Signs Of Health Part 1 92
    A1.3.5b Signs Of Health Part 2 93
    A1.3.6 Church's Profile 94
    A2.1.1a Steps To Influence 95
    A2.1.1b Steps To Influence Insights 96
    A2.1.3a A Clearly Focused Vision...97
    A2.1.3b Syndromes That Limit Your Vision 98
    A2.1.3c Selling The Vision..99
    A2.1.4 Clearly Established Goals 100
    A2.1.5 A Clearly Effective Strategy 101

    A2.2.1 Biblical Background 102
    A2.2.2 The Volunteer Principle 103
    A2.2.3 The Pareto Principle 80-20 104
    A2.3.1 The Evangelism Principle 105
    A2.3.2 "Reaching the Unchurched in The 2000'S" 106
    A2.3.3 Increasing Visitor Flow: Making Your List 107
    A2.5.3 Ideas for Meaningful Worship 108
    A2.6.1 The Finance Principle. 109
A2.7 Pastoral Care 110
A2.8 Discipleship 111
A2.9 Fellowship 112
A4.1a Discipline 1: Hiring Staff. 113
A4.1b Discipline 1 (Cont.): Hiring Staff 114
A4.1c Discipline 2: Conflict Management 115

APPENDIX 2 - ACTIVITIES 117
    Church Picnic 118
    Five, Ten, And Twenty Years Anniversary Celebrations. 118
    Independence Sunday 118
    Thanksgiving. 118
    Christmas 119
    Easter 119
    Ice Cream Social 119
    Sweetheart Banquet. 119
    Church Anniversary 119
    Find A Parade 120
    Renewing Your Vows 120

APPENDIX 3 - CELEBRATIONS 121
    Baptisms 122
    Commissioning Ministers 122
    Mother's Day 122
    Father's Day 122
    New Members. 123
    Certificate Of Recognition. 123
    Graduations 123
    Baby Dedications 123

ACKNOWLEDGEMENTS

To my Mom and Dad, I want to say "thank you" for giving me my first full-time job in ministry. You guys taught me how to love and be curious about people. Dad, you are the best pastor I know and my first pastor. Without your love and encouragement, I wouldn't be here nor would I have written *Balanced Church*.

To the first pastor I worked for who wasn't family, Tim Turner, I say thank you. You gave me my first exposure to the passion I had for administrative and leadership giftings. You took me to conferences that trained me on how to lead and organize, and for that, I am forever grateful. This work is because you helped me discover my gift.

To Conrad Lowe for leading a conference called Model Church in the late 80s and 90s that gave me not just principles, but helped me understand how to organize those principles for effective administration in the local church. Thank you for having lunch with me a couple of times so I could visit with you, and for granting me permission to share some of the material written in this resource. You have been a tremendous blessing in my life for many years.

To Maury Davis who taught me that anointing draws people, but administration keeps them. That awakened in me the passion and knowing that I had inside that God had given me the gifts of administration and leadership. Thank you for walking with me for many years as a pastor, mentor, coach, champion, and most importantly, friend.

To Drs. Sam and Brenda Chand and the team at Dream Releaser Coaching, Dr. Chris Bowen and Robin LaGrow. Each and every one of you awakened dreams inside of me that had long died. *Balanced Church* is one of those dreams that had long been buried in the files of my packed-up office. But this team awakened in me a passion to help pastors and business leaders with administration and organizational processes.

To the team at Four Rivers Media who walked this rookie author through this project. Thank you Martijn, John, Megan, Sarah, Debbie, and the rest of the team for working with me, cultivating in me a passion to get out what has been in me, and to make it a great resource for helping pastors in the US and globally.

PREFACE

Almost forty years ago, I began a journey in full-time ministry. Now, it was probably obvious that I would follow the footsteps of my dad, my grandfather, my Mamaw, and my great grandfather. I started in 1983 as an intern with my uncle then began full-time ministry with my dad. Ministry always interested me as I watched my mom, dad, and grandparents serve people.

I felt the call to ministry as a 17-year-old boy during camp, but the terminology then was "preaching." I will never forget telling my parents about God's calling on my life and from that point forward, I continued in ministry began from secular college to Bible college. I struggled with the meaning of being a "preacher" because I never felt called to preach, but to serve as a leader. I always felt drawn to work in the marketplace to make a living as a preacher. I felt drawn to the process, not the preaching. I could live without preaching but I couldn't live without organizing and developing.

So, I began ministry almost forty years ago with tension between the anointing and administration. I could sense the Spirit so strongly, but He always moved me to structure rather than speaking. But because speaking and preaching was the norm, I became a youth pastor. Most of my friends at the time had their eyes on being a senior pastor and being a youth pastor was the first step to getting there. The first eleven years, I served as an associate pastor to pastors at two churches. I absolutely loved helping them do the work of their ministry. I loved organizing and developing processes for reaching people, developing people, and helping organize services, teams, and office administration. I found myself fulfilled with watching a lead pastor become successful and helping them build a workable strategy for reaching and retaining people.

In my second tenure as a youth/music associate, I started attending seminars and leadership development events. At the time, John Maxwell was leaving Skyline Weslyan to start Injoy, and I was one of his first followers. I found myself digesting everything I could on leadership, team development, structure, administration, being a part of a growing church, and on and on the list goes.

PREFACE

In the late 80s and early 90s I settled into the fact that I would be an associate my whole life. Then in 1994, my trajectory changed and I suddenly become who I thought I never would become—Senior Pastor. I put into practice the things I had learned the previous eleven years of serving other pastors and the church became a burgeoning ministry in middle Tennessee.

At the end of that ministry, I wrote *Balanced Church*. I put together the contents of the book and manual that you will soon partake of. But in 2006, the dream the Lord put in my heart to help pastors was buried never to be awakened again. Buried in boxes and boxes, My dreams, knowledge, insights, and experiences became radio silent.

But late last year that dream reawakened. Through various events in my life, I began to dream again about helping churches as an older, experienced minister with the gift of administration that God had given me. You see, when I pray, I don't get charged about preaching another sermon or giving another talk. I get excited and absolutely elated at the possibility of helping highly anointed and gifted preachers and pastors who hate administration create ways to plan the details of administration so they can catch a vision and preach the message that is a fire shut up in their bones. You are capable of doing less of what you hate and more of what you love and were created to do by doing what I love and was created to do—take the things you don't want to do from you through the *Balanced Church* process. In my mother's womb, God created me to shepherd you in reorganizing the structural and administrative processes of your church.

The second reason for this book and manual is to set some young ministers and even older ministers free who wonder why they never loved the preaching. It is okay to love the process and structure because you were made for that role. You don't have to be the "main guy," you are just as valuable as his or her right hand.

It is my dream to make your dreams for your church become a reality. My prayer is that *Balanced Church* will help you do just that.

INTRODUCTION

I have always been interested and fascinated with the local church. All of my life, I have visited, observed, volunteered, led, and studied local church leadership and ministry. Throughout, I have always wondered why some churches grow and others do not. I have often asked myself, "Why do many of the men and women I meet seem to believe that the final destination for ministry is becoming the senior pastor?" Most of the ministers I served at that time had never served as an associate pastor for another pastor. Most of the older ministers I have known, including in my family line, were all senior pastors of churches, but the majority of them expressed how they wished they had learned under someone before being over someone. I believe it was a generational thing.

But growing up in that generation, I always felt pressure to be the lead pastor. I always felt the push that if you wanted to be someone in ministry you had to be the main pastor—the associate and administrative roles were less anointed. Even in recent years, I have had many ask me, "Why do you want to be an Executive Pastor instead of the lead pastor?" They added, "You are so good as a leader. You will answer to God for not accepting the responsibility He has called you to accept.

What if I proposed that, even in the Old Testament, God had more priests who served in setting up the tabernacle, temple, and place of worship and only a minority who served as the High Priest? Is it possible that in the New Testament, we see there are many associate roles than only the pastor of the church? Could the reason some do not function well in the calling be because they have never been encouraged to do so?

The idea of a balanced church is that the anointing of God draws people in, and the gifts of administration build systems and structures to keep them there. I have a strong conviction that the local church is missing the balance between Spirit and structure. I am amazed that some of the most anointed men and women I have ever seen or heard have a passion to grow their churches, but it remains only a passion and not a reality because they have never had an administrative coach help them build a plan to retain those drawn.

INTRODUCTION

You see, that's where I was until the late '80s. I always desired to help the church and the Kingdom of God grow but I didn't understand the concept of administration. I didn't understand the concept of assessment, alignment, application, and accountability all working together with the spontaneity of the Holy Spirit to successfully execute a replicable plan for effective preaching and ministering.

I believe the Lord led me to *Balanced Church* to better understand how to help ministries and ministers build an operating system that formulates what is visibly happening in the ministry. I have worked hard over the last thirty years to develop this process. I have executed it in the ministries I have had the opportunity to serve in from church planter, turnaround pastor, Executive Pastor of two megachurches, and associate pastor. I have also used the components of *Balanced Church* to lead nonprofits, help business owners build their businesses, and serve in the marketplace. I have taught these principles to younger men than I and have seen them go to exponentially larger ministries than I, but the operating system is still the same.

In the following pages, I will walk you through five modules, each containing components that are vital to retaining the harvest, growth, and profit that God wants to bless your ministry with. It is my privilege to help you unpack these essential principles that I believe have been proven to grow the Kingdom of God. In answering the call of God, I am passionate about equipping you to exponentially grow and impact the culture of your ministry.

It is possible to reassign the things you hate to do in order to focus on what you love to do. There is a way to create a plan and apply those principles so they move forward through training and planning. But this is not for the faint of heart. Growing a ministry and the Kingdom is not an easy path, or everybody and every church would be doing it. It takes dedication to follow a time-tested plan and then executing the plan with a seasoned coach.

It is my joy to walk alongside you as you become a balanced church. I look forward to being a part of your personal growth and growth in your church attendance, finances, volunteers, leaders, and community influence. I am excited that you have chosen *Balanced Church*. Let's begin the exciting journey of change and transition and get ready to enter into a brand-new ministry.

WHAT IS A BALANCED CHURCH?

1) A church with an inspiring vision

2) A church with exciting goals

3) A church with practical, proven strategies

4) A church with a pastor who leads

5) A church with a ministering congregation

6) A church with a plan that works

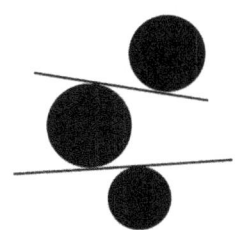

MODULE 1

ASSESSMENTS

"Understanding where you are today in order to get to where you want to be tomorrow."

MODULE 1

1.1 ASSESSING THE PASTOR

1.1.1 Leadership Hints

The Senior Pastor is the _____ and the
_____ for a solid, balanced church.

10 HELPFUL HINTS

1) Be a _____.

2) Be a _____.

3) Be a _____.

4) Be a _____.

5) Be a _____.

6) Be a _____.

7) Be a _____.

8) Be a _____.

9) Be a _____.

10) Be a _____.

ASSESSMENTS

1.1.2 Pastor's Profile

Personality _____

Spiritual Gift(s) _____

_____

_____

_____

Passion _____

_____

_____

_____

1.2 ASSESSING YOUR STAFF

1.2.1 Staff Profile

Personality _____

Spiritual Gift(s) _____

_____

_____

_____

Passion _____

_____

_____

_____

1.3 ASSESSING YOUR CHURCH

1.3.1 Each Church is Different

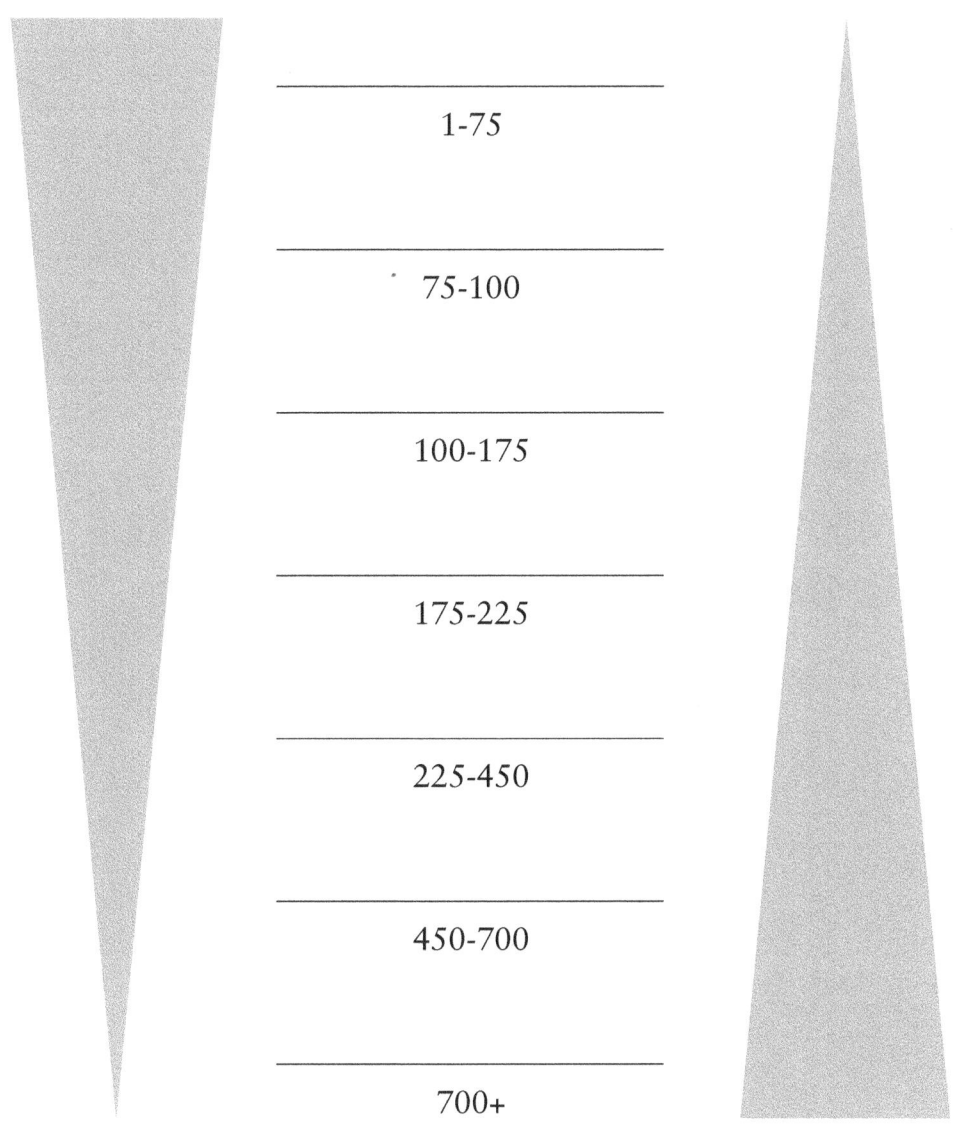

1-75

75-100

100-175

175-225

225-450

450-700

700+

1.3.2 When a Church Grows

1) The pastor's hands on ministry _____ and the congregation's hands on ministry _____.

2) The pastor's and congregation's gifts become _____.

3) The _____ and the _____ _____ of ministry increase.

4) Ministry and influence _____ between the pastor and the congregation.

5) Biblical philosophy is _____.

6) _____ + _____ = _____.

ASSESSMENTS

1.3.3 Ministry Standing

1.3.3a Where Does Your Ministry Stand? Part 1

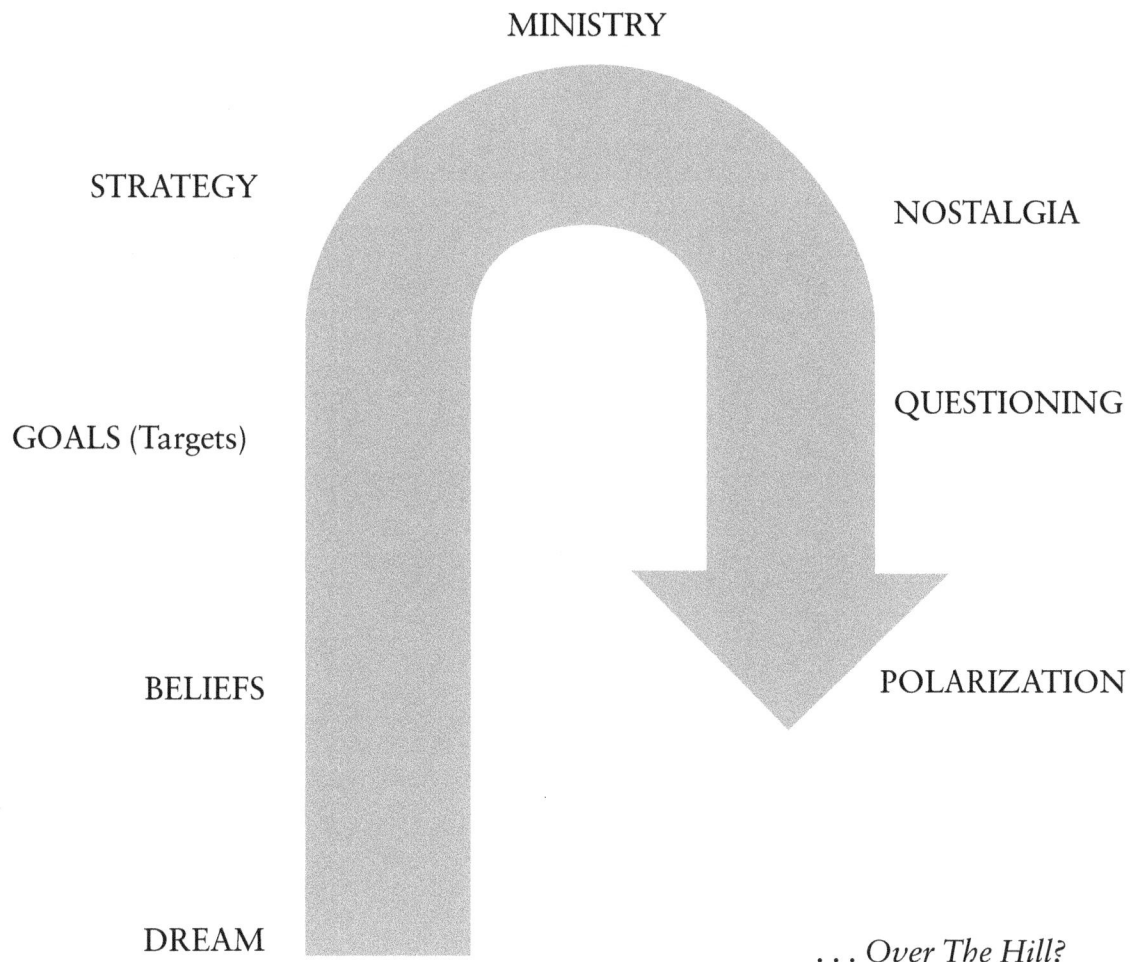

Church's Health Cycle Model

On The Edge . . .

MINISTRY

STRATEGY

NOSTALGIA

QUESTIONING

GOALS (Targets)

BELIEFS

POLARIZATION

DREAM

. . . Over The Hill?

1.3.3b Where Does Your Ministry Stand? Part 2

Church's Health Cycle Model

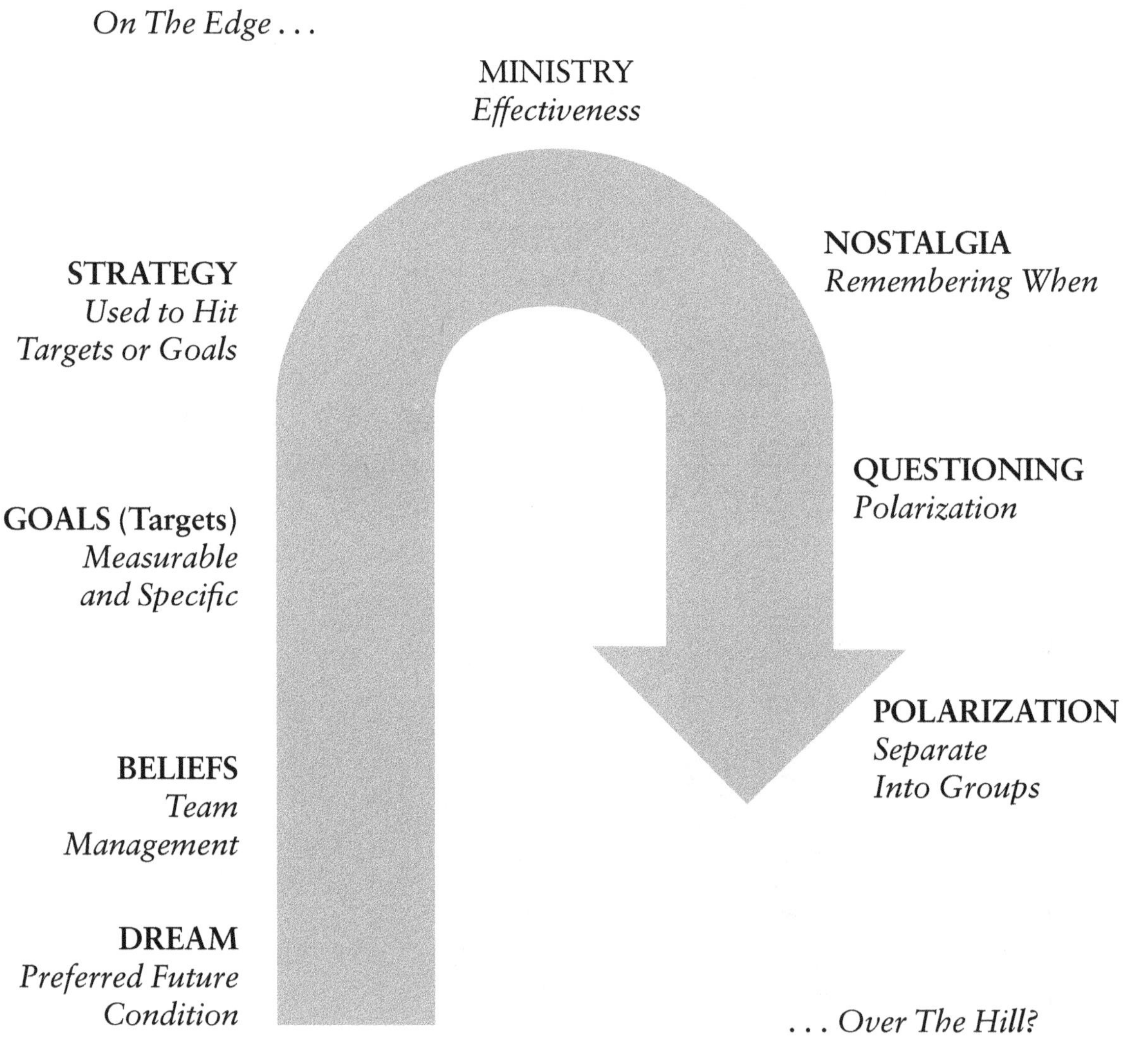

On The Edge . . .

MINISTRY
Effectiveness

STRATEGY
*Used to Hit
Targets or Goals*

NOSTALGIA
Remembering When

QUESTIONING
Polarization

GOALS (Targets)
*Measurable
and Specific*

POLARIZATION
*Separate
Into Groups*

BELIEFS
*Team
Management*

DREAM
*Preferred Future
Condition*

. . . Over The Hill?

ASSESSMENTS

1.3.3c Where Does Your Ministry Stand? Part 3

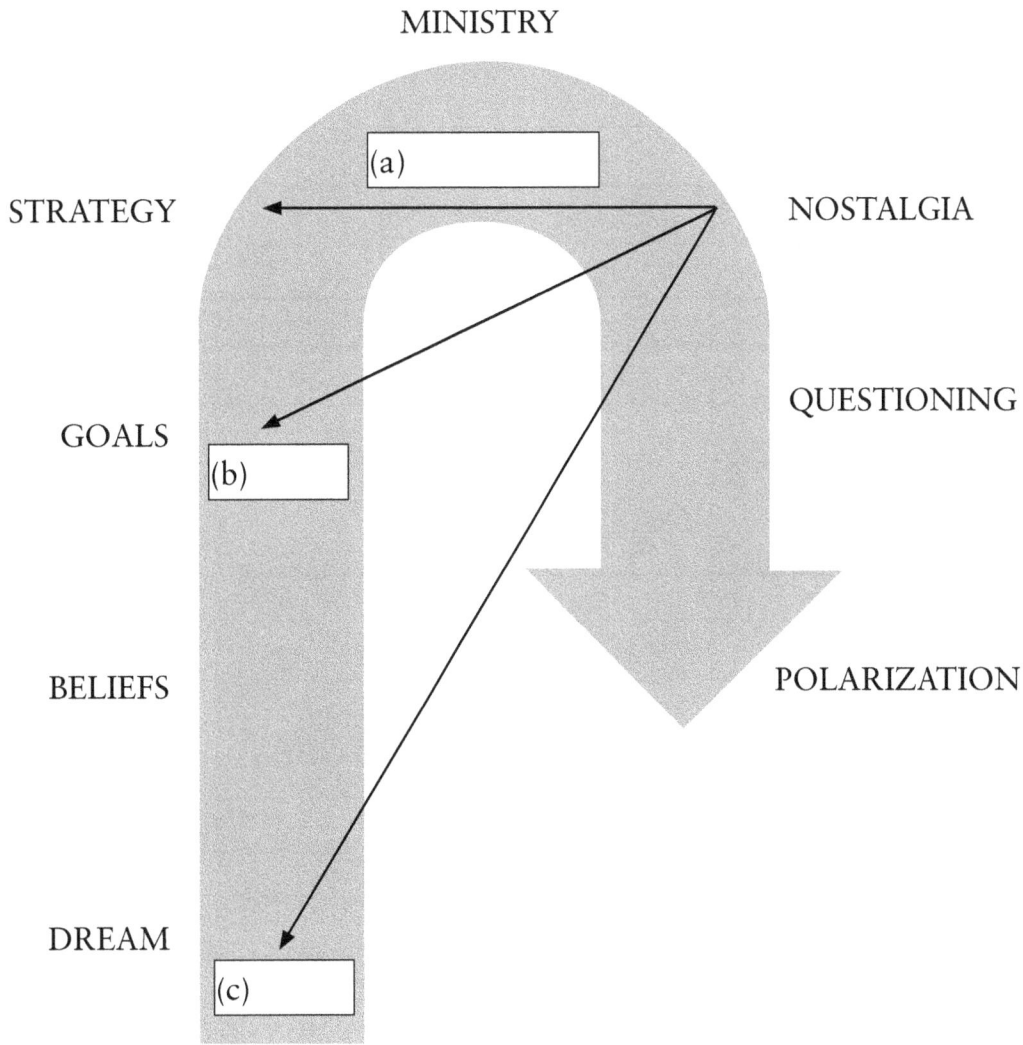

Church's Health Cycle Model

MODULE 1

1.3.4 Church Illness

1.3.4a Signs of Illness Part 1

	TREND	
	YES	NO
1) Maintenance Complex _____ _____ _____ _____		
2) Failure Syndrome _____ _____ _____ _____		
3) Credibility Gap _____ _____ _____ _____		
4) Fellowshipitis _____ _____ _____ _____		

ASSESSMENTS

1.3.4b Signs of Illness Part 2

	TREND	
	YES	NO
1) People Blindness _____ _____ _____ _____		
2) Overcrowding _____ _____ _____ _____		
3) Leadership Tensions _____ _____ _____ _____		
4) Old Age _____ _____ _____ _____		

MODULE 1

1.3.5 Church Health

1.3.5a Signs of Health Part 1

	TREND	
	YES	NO
1) Effective Leadership		
2) Agreed Agenda		
3) Believing Prayer		
4) Life-Related Bible Teaching		

1.3.5b Signs of Health Part 2

	TREND	
	YES	NO
1) Mobilized Membership _____ _____ _____ _____		
2) Community Minded _____ _____ _____ _____		
3) Ongoing Evangelism _____ _____ _____ _____		
4) New Member Incorporation _____ _____ _____ _____		

MODULE 1

1.3.6 Church's Profile

Church's condition: Growing

                                     Plateaued

                                     Declining

Church's category: _____

Where does your ministry stand? _____

Signs of Illness:

1) _____

2) _____

3) _____

Signs of Health:

1) _____

2) _____

3) _____

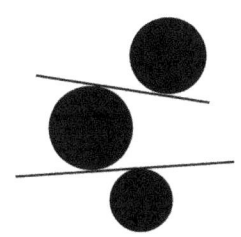

MODULE 2

ALL IMPORTANT COMPONENTS FOR GROWTH

"If you don't know the ingredients to make a great product, you work in vain."

MODULE 2

2.1 LEADERSHIP

2.1.1a Steps to Influence

```
                                              PERSON
                                    PERSONNEL
                          PRODUCTION
               PERMISSION
   POSITION
```

Step 1.   People follow you because _____
          _____

Step 2.   People follow you because _____
          _____

Step 3.   People follow you because _____
          _____

Step 4.   People follow you because _____
          _____

Step 5.   People follow you because _____
          _____

2.1.1b Steps to Influence Insights

1) The higher the steps the _____.

2) The higher the steps the _____.

3) The higher the steps the _____.

4) The higher the steps the _____.

5) The higher the steps the _____.

MODULE 2

2.1.2 The Big Picture

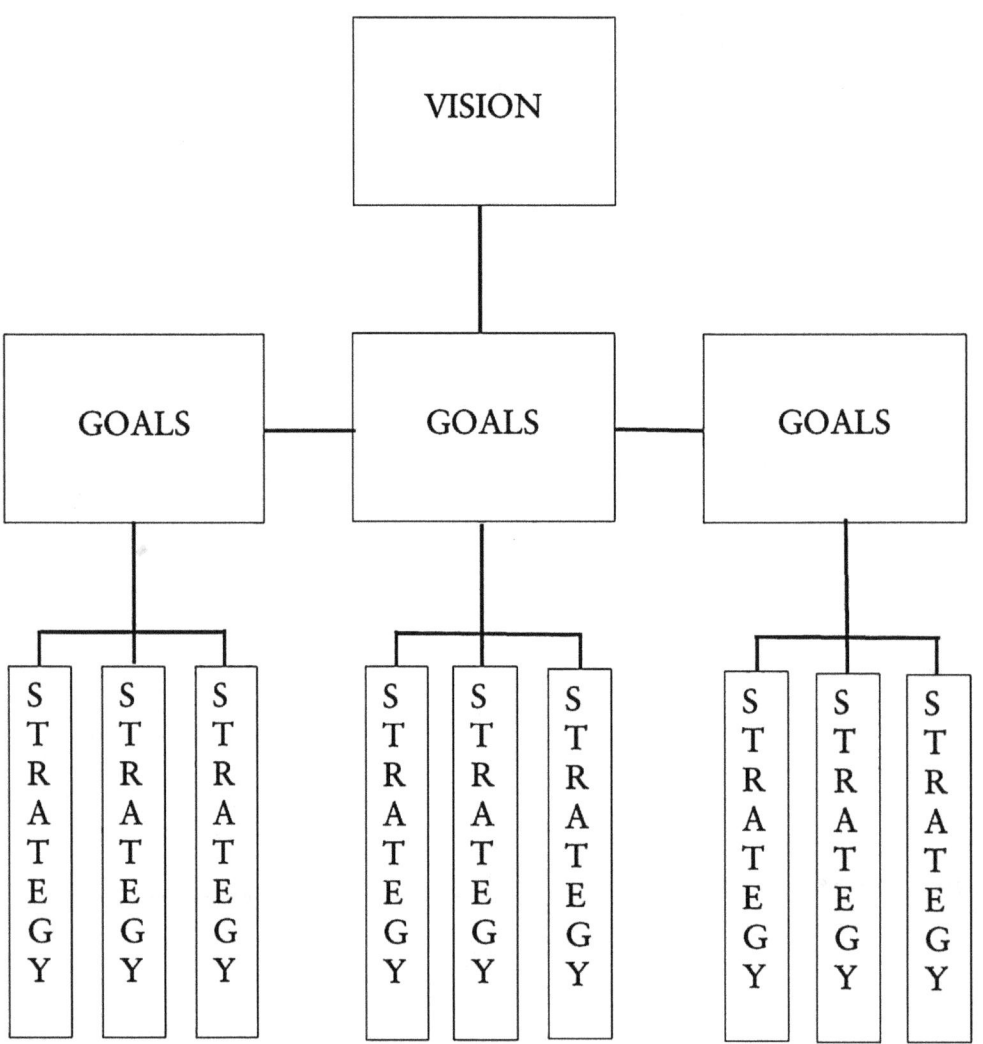

2.1.3 Vision For Growth

2.1.3a A Clearly Focused Vision

A growing church has a detailed description of the preferred future condition

Definition: A more specific picture of what your church must be in order to accomplish its purpose.

The benefits of a clear vision statement are:

1) It will give us _____.

2) It will keep our _____ in order.

3) It will build _____ and _____.

Examples:

> **Our Vision**
>
> Reaching the Lost.
>
>   Equipping the Found.
>
>   Aiming for Excellence.
>
>   Leading Responsibly.

MODULE 2

2.1.3b Syndromes That Limit Your Vision

A) Problem Solving Syndrome

When more time is spent _____ than leading.

B) Busy Enough Now Syndrome

When your ability to lead is limited by a _____.

"Are you doing things right . . . or doing the right things?"

C) No Vacancy Syndrome

When you become so content with the _____ you have, you don't see the need to bring more in.

D) Nostalgia Syndrome

When you spend more time remembering the _____ than you do preparing for the future.

E) The Lazarus Syndrome

When you spend too much time and energy attempting to recover _____ members.

2.1.3c Selling The Vision

A) Preparing

    1) _____ Priorities

      a) The Great Commission

      b) The Great Commandment

    2) _____ Strengths

    3) _____ Gifts

    4) _____ Opportunities

B) Presenting

    1) _____

    2) _____

"Not much happens without a dream. And for something great to happen there must always be a great dream. Behind every great achievement is a dreamer of great dreams. Much more than a dream is required to bring it to reality; but the dream must be there first." —Robert Greenleaf

2.1.4 Clearly Established Goals

A growing church has detailed targets that will accomplish its vision and purpose.

Definition: A specific target.

1) The goal should be _____.

2) The goal should be _____.

3) The goal should be _____.

4) The goal should be _____.

5) The goal should be _____.

2.1.5 A Clearly Effective Strategy

A growing church will use the most practical,

proven tools to accomplish its goals.

Definition: A detailed course of action that moves a church to achieving its goals.

1) A strategy should match the unique _____ of each congregation.

2) A strategy should match the _____ of each congregation.

EXAMPLE

<u>GOAL</u>: To increase finances 20%

<u>STRATEGY</u>: One month of stewardship climaxing with God's Guarantee

---

On a scale of 1-10, rate your leadership:

1   2   3   4   5   6   7   8   9   10

The vision for the church where I serve is:

_____

_____

_____

Goals for the church where I serve are:

_____

_____

_____

MODULE 2

2.2 VOLUNTEERISM

2.2.1 Biblical Background

FOR VOLUNTEERS

(Acts 6:1-7)

Observations:

1 (vs. 1) _____

2 (vs. 2) _____

3 (vs. 3, 4) _____

4 (vs. 5) _____

5 (vs. 6) _____

6 (vs. 7) _____

Conclusion: The more qualified volunteers who minister, the greater the growth of the church.

2.2.2 The Volunteer Principle

A growing church needs to mobilize its members to active service for Christ in accordance with their gifts.

```
┌─────────────────────────┐
│         STAFF           │
└─────────────────────────┘

┌─────────────────────────┐
│        LEADERS          │
└─────────────────────────┘

┌─────────────────────────┐
│       VOLUNTEERS        │
└─────────────────────────┘
```

(STAFF)   1) Set the _____

(STAFF)   2) Recruit and train _____

(LEADERS)   3) Recruit and train _____

(VOLUNTEERS)   4) Perform the _____

(BOTH)   5) Establish _____

2.2.3 The Pareto Principle
80-20

To grow, a pastor must invest 80% of his time into the 20% who produce 80% of the work.

_____ of the people produce _____ of the results.
_____ of the people produce _____ of the results.

MAINTENANCE ORGANIZATION

PASTOR	Serves the _____.	VOLUNTEER
20%	Do _____ of the work.	VOLUNTEER
80%	Do _____ of the work.	VOLUNTEER

GROWING ORGANIZATION

PASTOR	Equips the _____ of the time. Serves the _____ of the time.	MODELER
20%	Are equipped to lead the _____.	VOLUNTEER
80%	Do the ministry of the church.	VOLUNTEER

ALL IMPORTANT COMPONENTS FOR GROWTH

2.2.4 Passion

What is something you really enjoy doing?

(i.e. teaching children, working in the garden, drama, recreation, etc.)

_____
_____
_____
_____
_____
_____
_____
_____
_____
_____
_____
_____
_____
_____

This is an easy one . . . don't make it hard!

MODULE 2

2.2.5 Volunteer Profile

Personality _____

Spiritual Gift(s) _____

_____

_____

Passion _____

_____

_____

_____

2.2.6 Generational Differences
Balanced Church

There must be consideration given to the generational differences found in many churches. Now some churches have chosen to be very demographically controlled but for the majority of churches in America, we find generational variety.

So, as we move to the various components of *Balanced Church*, let's give consideration to these differences.

GENERATION	DIFFERENCES
Greatest Generation	Born 1901-1924
Aspiration	Home Ownership
Attitude Toward Technology	Largely disengaged
Attitude Toward Career	Jobs are for life
Signature Product	Automobile
Communication Media	Formal Letter
Communication Preference	Face to Face
Financial Decisions	Face to Face
Baby Boomers	1945-1963
Aspiration	Job Security
Attitude Toward Technology	Early IT adaptors
Attitude Toward Career	Careers are defined by employers
Signature Product	Television
Communication Media	Telephone
Communication Preference	Face-to-face ideally, but telephone or email if required
Financial Decisions	Face-to-face but increasingly will go online

MODULE 2

GENERATION	DIFFERENCES
Generation X	**1964-1980**
Aspiration	Work-Life Balance
Attitude Toward Technology	Digital immigrants
Attitude Toward Career	Portfolio Careers – Loyal to profession, not employers
Signature Product	Personal Computer
Communication Media	Email and Text Message
Communication Preference	Text messages or email
Financial Decisions	Online, but would prefer face-to-face if time permits
Generation Y	**1981-1995**
Aspiration	Freedom and Flexibility
Attitude Toward Technology	Digital Natives
Attitude Toward Career	Digital entrepreneurs working with organizations, not for them
Signature Product	Tablet/Smartphone
Communication Media	Text or Social Media
Communication Preference	Online and mobile (text messaging)
Financial Decisions	Face-to-face
Generation Z	**Born After 1995**
Aspiration	Security and stability
Attitude Toward Technology	Technoholics entirely dependent on IT, limited grasp of alternative
Attitude Toward Career	Career multitaskers move seamlessly between businesses
Signature Product	3D printing, driverless cars
Communication Media	Hand-held devices or integrated into closing
Communication Preference	FaceTime, Zoom
Financial Decisions	Solutions will be digitally crowd-sourced

ALL IMPORTANT COMPONENTS FOR GROWTH

2.3 EVANGELISM

2.3.1 The Evangelism Principle

A growing church must incorporate evangelism into every area of ministry programming.

Step 1 _____ Develop a prospect list of potential new members.

Step 2 _____ Enlist members with the spiritual gift of intercessory prayer to pray for all visitors, prospects, and those who will be going to the homes of potential new members.

Step 3 _____ Follow Up!
Follow Up!
Follow Up!

KEYS TO SUCCESS:

- Think like an unchurched person
- Design intentional evangelism into your programming
- Elevate the role of evangelism in your congregation

MODULE 2

2.3.2 "Reaching the Unchurched in The 2000's"

In order for the church to effectively evangelize America, we must understand it has to be a multi-generational approach.

Some important facts:

1) _____

2) _____

3) _____

4) _____

As these generations are reaching middle age, their interest in the church is increasing.

Why?

1) _____

2) _____

3) _____

2.3.3 Increasing Visitor Flow: Making Your List

| STEP 1 | Advertising _____ |

| STEP 2 | Programming _____ |

| STEP 3 | Inviting _____ |

MODULE 2

2.3.4 Inviting

2.3.4a What Visitors See

Taking a close look at your church through the eyes of a visitor.

STEP 1

Select a committee to include:

A) Long-term members (10+ years)

B) Medium-term members (5+ years)

C) Short-term members (2+ years)

STEP 2

Plan four weekly meetings to discuss:
1) What Brought You?
   Receiving personal experiences of your becoming acquainted with this church.

2) What Kept You?
   Review what influenced you to stay and join this church.

3) What Did You See?
   Make a photographic tour beginning from your car when you first see the church through Sunday School and worship until your car leaves the parking lot. (Take at least 24 pictures.)

4) What Would You Change?
   Consider areas that could be improved for the unchurched visitor.

2.3.4b Visitor's Welcome Center

PURPOSE: This center will be staffed with friendly members of your church, who will greet all visitors (or return visitors), distribute helpful information, escort them to the appropriate location and most importantly . . . get their name, address, and phone number.

STEP 1	Recruit greeters who are friendly, outgoing, and convey a positive attitude.
STEP 2	Provide classroom training to assure that each greeter has a clear understanding of this new "outreach tool."
STEP 3	Design materials that will be helpful to a visitor. (Ex. Map, schedule, church brochure, letter from the pastor, etc.)
STEP 4	Purchase a guest register or have an attractive form for each visitor to fill out.
STEP 5	Locate your Welcome Center in the most central and visible area of your church. Hang a large banner that identifies the Welcome Center.
STEP 6	Publicly dedicate the Welcome Center and commission the staff of greeters.
STEP 7	Meet together with all members every two months for the purpose of celebration, evaluation, and rescheduling.

MODULE 2

2.3.5 "Make Your List" Strategies

Select possible strategies to "Make Your List"[1] during the *Balanced Church* Year.

ADVERTISING:

    1) Building Signs _____

    2) Radio _____

    3) New Resident (everybody) _____

    4) Newspaper _____

PROGRAMMING:

    1) Seminars _____

    2) Test Waters _____

    3) Concerts _____

INVITING:

    1) What Visitors See _____

    2) Baptism Invitation Cards _____

    3) Test Waters _____

    4) Special Delivery Letters _____

---

[1] Dr. John Maxwell, Injoy Ministries.

2.4 ASSIMILATION

2.4.1 Assimilation Process

GROWTH TRACK

PASTOR'S NEWCOMER CLASS	SMALL GROUP	DREAM TEAM
13 weeks	52 weeks	Lifetime

GOALS:

1) Relationship

2) Ministry

2.4.2 Growth Track

1) Vision

2) Doctrine & History

3) Membership

4) Ministry Placement

ALL IMPORTANT COMPONENTS FOR GROWTH

2.5 WORSHIP

2.5.1 Transitional Mindsets[2]

TRADITIONAL CHURCH		GROWING CHURCH
Worship	HOPE →	Celebration
Fellowship	RELATIONAL SKILLS → Need to know they are cared for Happens outside the walls	Intensive Care
Education	RELATIONSHIPS → Do they love each other? Changed lives	Small Groups

---

[2] Carl George, *Fuller Institute*.

2.5.2 Positive, Uplifting Worship

82% of visitors rate this as the most important reason for joining a church.

| STEP 1 | Promote a family feeling with warmth and flexibility. |

| STEP 2 | Share joys and concerns by praying for needs and two minute prepared testimony of victory. |

| STEP 3 | Emphasize family values with a children's sermon or children's church. |

| STEP 4 | Use humor or illustration every 7 1/2 minutes. |

| STEP 5 | Accelerate the temp of the music, sing familiar hymns, and make special music as professional as possible. |

ALL IMPORTANT COMPONENTS FOR GROWTH

2.5.3 Ideas For Meaningful Worship

- What steps can I take to add celebration, hope, and "success" to my worship?

___

- If we are 80% full, what is our plan to provide more space for growth?

___

- What steps can we take to offer a full music program?

___

2.6 STEWARDSHIP

2.6.1 The Finance Principle[3]

A growing church must have adequate financial resources to underwrite growth expenses.

KEY RATIO: _____ out of every _____ in total church budget should be designated for outreach (NOT missions!)

1) _____ comes from leadership, people involved in ministry, and exciting ideas

_____.

"People will pay for whatever they value!"

_____.

_____.

2) Financial growth _____ people growth.

_____.

_____.

3) Raising the finances gives you the _____ to determine how they will be allocated.

_____.

---
3 John Maxwell, Injoy Ministries ***

2.7 PASTORAL CARE

The Pastor or Pastoral staff will never be _____

to take care of the needs of the congregation.

There must be a system in place in case you _____.

There are a variety of opportunities to provide pastoral care:

1) P _____

2) S _____ G _____

3) B _____ & L _____ T _____

4) A _____ G _____

5) M _____ T _____

Just Remember:

You are not the _____!

So recruit and train _____!

2.8 DISCIPLESHIP

The Great Commission calls us to make _____, not just _____.

If you will keep focused on growing _____ and not just growing a _____; then you will see the natural byproduct that is larger than _____.

DISCIPLESHIP INVOLVES:

1) _____

2) _____

3) _____

4) _____

It just takes _____!

2.9 FELLOWSHIP

"And they devoted themselves to the apostles' teaching and the fellowship, to the breaking of bread and the prayers. And awe came upon every soul, and many wonders and signs were being done through the apostles. And all who believed were together and had all things in common. And they were selling their possessions and belongings and distributing the proceeds to all, as any had need. And day by day, attending the temple together and breaking bread in their homes, they received their food with glad and generous hearts, praising God and having favor with all the people. And the Lord added to their number day by day those who were being saved."

—Acts 2:42–47 (ESV)

Fellowship in the building of _____.

Fellowship is the intentional pursuit of _____.

Fellowship is the passionate calling to _____.

Fellowship is the directive for _____.

"And let us consider one another in order to stir up love and good works, not forsaking the assembling of ourselves together, as is the manner of some, but exhorting one another, and so much the more as you see the Day approaching."

—Hebrews 10:24, 25 (NKJV)

Fellowship is the responsibility of a _____

to _____ with other believers.

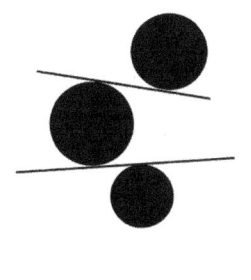

MODULE 3

APPLICATION YEAR CALENDAR

MODULE 3

JANUARY

BC Project: Activity:

Sermon Series: Celebrations:

SUNDAY	MONDAY	TUESDAY	WEDNESDAY	THURSDAY	FRIDAY	SATURDAY

APPLICATION YEAR CALENDAR

FEBRUARY

BC Project: _____

Activity: _____

Sermon Series: _____

Celebrations: _____

SUNDAY	MONDAY	TUESDAY	WEDNESDAY	THURSDAY	FRIDAY	SATURDAY

MODULE 3

MARCH

BC Project: _____

Activity: _____

Sermon Series: _____

Celebrations: _____

SUNDAY	MONDAY	TUESDAY	WEDNESDAY	THURSDAY	FRIDAY	SATURDAY

APPLICATION YEAR CALENDAR

APRIL

BC Project: _____

Activity: _____

Sermon Series: _____

Celebrations: _____

SUNDAY	MONDAY	TUESDAY	WEDNESDAY	THURSDAY	FRIDAY	SATURDAY

MODULE 3

MAY

BC Project: _____

Activity: _____

Sermon Series: _____

Celebrations: _____

SUNDAY	MONDAY	TUESDAY	WEDNESDAY	THURSDAY	FRIDAY	SATURDAY

APPLICATION YEAR CALENDAR

JUNE

BC Project: _____

Activity: _____

Sermon Series: _____

Celebrations: _____

SUNDAY	MONDAY	TUESDAY	WEDNESDAY	THURSDAY	FRIDAY	SATURDAY

MODULE 3

JULY

BC Project: _____

Activity: _____

Sermon Series: _____

Celebrations: _____

SUNDAY	MONDAY	TUESDAY	WEDNESDAY	THURSDAY	FRIDAY	SATURDAY

APPLICATION YEAR CALENDAR

AUGUST

BC Project: _____

Activity: _____

Sermon Series: _____

Celebrations: _____

SUNDAY	MONDAY	TUESDAY	WEDNESDAY	THURSDAY	FRIDAY	SATURDAY

MODULE 3

SEPTEMBER

BC Project: _____   Activity: _____

Sermon Series: _____   Celebrations: _____

SUNDAY	MONDAY	TUESDAY	WEDNESDAY	THURSDAY	FRIDAY	SATURDAY

APPLICATION YEAR CALENDAR

OCTOBER

BC Project: _____

Activity: _____

Sermon Series: _____

Celebrations: _____

SUNDAY	MONDAY	TUESDAY	WEDNESDAY	THURSDAY	FRIDAY	SATURDAY

MODULE 3

NOVEMBER

BC Project: _____

Activity: _____

Sermon Series: _____

Celebrations: _____

SUNDAY	MONDAY	TUESDAY	WEDNESDAY	THURSDAY	FRIDAY	SATURDAY

APPLICATION YEAR CALENDAR

DECEMBER

BC Project: _____

Activity: _____

Sermon Series: _____

Celebrations: _____

SUNDAY	MONDAY	TUESDAY	WEDNESDAY	THURSDAY	FRIDAY	SATURDAY

BALANCED CHURCH PLANNER

JANUARY

a
b
c
d

FEBRUARY

a
b
c
d

MARCH

a
b
c
d

APRIL

a
b
c
d

MAY

a
b
c
d

JUNE

a
b
c
d

JULY

a
b
c
d

AUGUST

a
b
c
d

SEPTEMBER

a
b
c
d

OCTOBER

a
b
c
d

NOVEMBER

a
b
c
d

DECEMBER

a
b
c
d

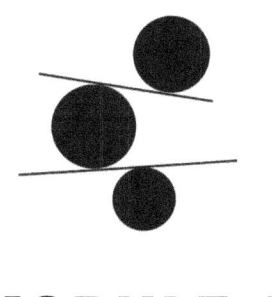

MODULE 4

ACQUIRED DISCIPLINES

MODULE 4

4.1 STAFF AND STAFFING RELATIONSHIPS DISCIPLINES

4.1a Discipline 1: Hiring Staff

If you are going to grow a church, you can't be a _____.

You will have to have _____.

Hiring staff members requires:

1) P _____

2) S _____

3) R _____

4) M _____

5) V _____

6) T _____

Where can you find good staff members?

1) In your _____

2) _____ you've developed.

3) _____

4) Other _____

Two keys for finding and developing good staff:

1) P _____

2) P _____

4.1b Discipline 1 (Cont.): Hiring Staff

THE FOUR C'S OF HIRING GREAT STAFF:

1) _____ – Are they godly and are they good?

2) _____ – Do they meet the job requirements and can they do the job?

3) _____ – Can they work with others?

4) _____ – Do they fit the environment and atmosphere of your church and office?

MODULE 4

4.1c Discipline 2: Conflict Management

Conflict in a church or business is _____.

Everyone is _____ in how they handle conflict and how they _____ to conflict.

    a) _____

    b) _____

Knowing your _____ is _____.

Get the _____ together.

Based on the different _____ involved determines how you _____ the particular situation.

_____ will only cause more and maybe bigger _____.

Go into the conflict with _____ and _____.

Love them the next time you _____ them.

Don't _____ people in conflict in the _____.

Don't make it _____ even though it can be.

MODULE 5

CONTINUED ACCOUNTABILITY RELATIONSHIP

Coaches

Mentors

Counselors

APPENDIX 1

ANSWER SHEETS

APPENDIX 1

A1.1.1 Leadership Hints

The Senior Pastor is the **visionary** and the **leader** for a solid, balanced church.

10 HELPFUL HINTS

1) Be a **vision caster**.

2) Be a **problem solver**.

3) Be a **communicator**.

4) Be **authentic**.

5) Be **proactive**.

6) Be **humble**.

7) Be **loving**.

8) Be **truthful**.

9) Be **faithful**.

10) Be **available**.

A1.3.1 Each Church Is Different

PASTOR — Responsibilities

PEOPLE — Responsibilities

CAT
1-75

DOG
75-100

CABIN
100-175

HOUSE
175-225

MANSION
225-450

CITY
450-700

NATION
700+

A1.3.2 When A Church Grows

1) The pastor's hands on ministry **decreases** and the congregation's hands on ministry **increases**.

2) The pastor's and congregation's gifts become **more clearly defined**.

3) The **quantity** and the **quality** of ministry increase.

4) Ministry and influence **shift** between the pastor and the congregation.

5) Biblical philosophy is **re-established**.

6) **LEADERSHIP** + **VOLUNTEERS** = **GROWTH**.

A1.3.3c Where Does Your Ministry Stand?

PART 3

Church's Health Cycle Model

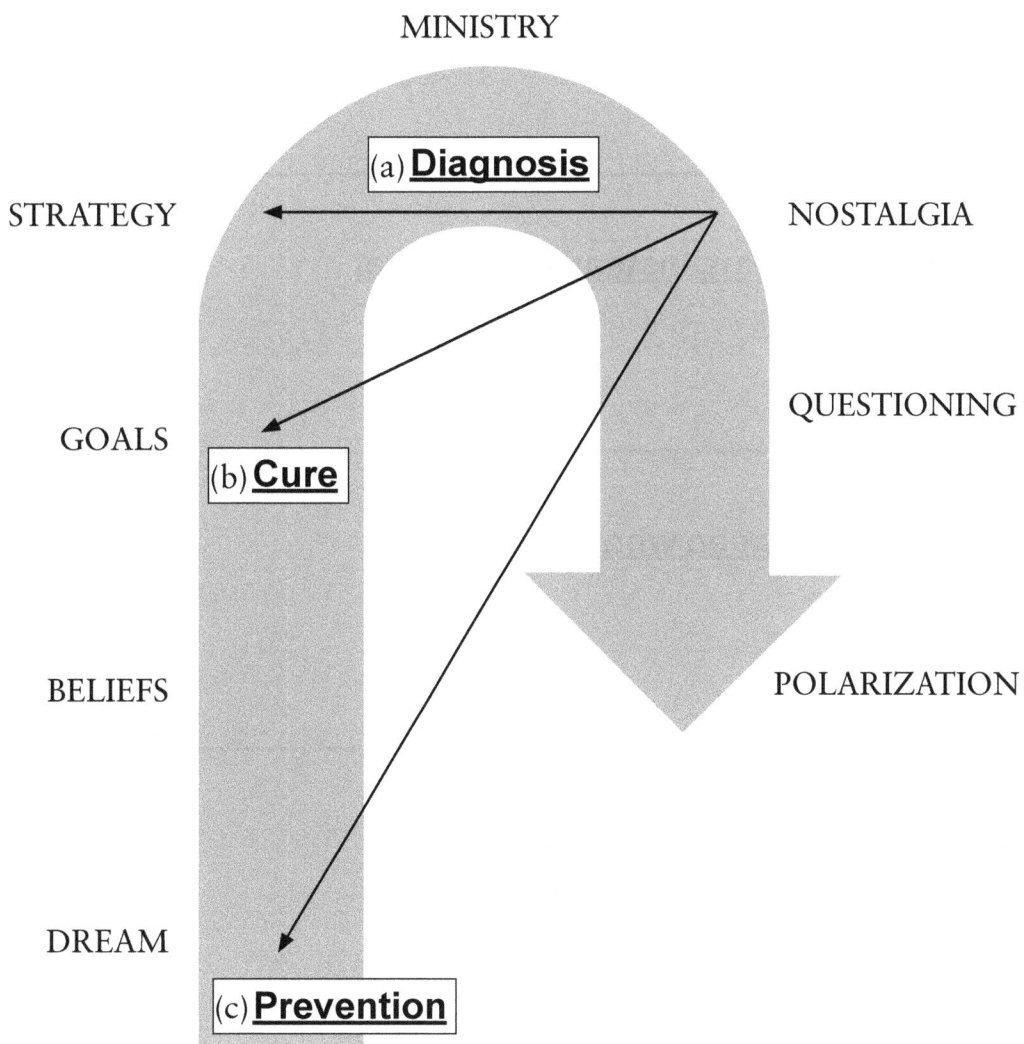

APPENDIX 1

A1.3.4a Signs Of Illness Part 1

	TREND	
	YES	NO
1) Maintenance Complex **Preoccupation with institutional survival**		
2) Failure Syndrome **Focusing on problems instead of potential**		
3) Credibility Gap **The difference between what you say and what you do**		
4) Fellowshipitis **Too much emphasis on fellowships and being close**		

ANSWER SHEETS

A1.3.4b Signs Of Illness Part 2

	TREND	
	YES	NO
1) People Blindness **Insensitivity to the needs of the people around the church**		
2) Overcrowding **Failure to plan for adequate ministries and facilities 80% implementation**		
3) Leadership Tensions **Management problems**		
4) Old Age **When the average age of the membership increases**		

APPENDIX 1

A1.3.5a Signs Of Health Part 1

	TREND	
	YES	NO
1) Effective Leadership **Where the vision is clear, the potential is identified, and the ministry is shared.**		
2) Agreed Agenda **When 80% of the membership share a vision.**		
3) Believing Prayer **Prayer undergirds every ministry of the church.**		
4) Life-Related Bible Teaching **Every lesson and sermon has practical application.**		

A1.3.5b Signs Of Health Part 2

	TREND	
	YES	NO
1) Mobilized Membership **Discover the gifts of the congregation and equip them for ministry**		
2) Community Minded **Service-oriented**		
3) Ongoing Evangelism **Every ministry and activity move the church toward the goal of evangelism.**		
4) New Member Incorporation **Begins with initial welcome, builds relationships, and ends with ministry involvement.**		

APPENDIX 1

A1.3.6 Church's Profile

Church's condition: Growing

Plateaued

Declining

Church's category: **Mansion**

Where does your ministry stand? **Beliefs**

Signs of Illness:

1) **Credibility Gap**

2) **Fellowshipitis**

3) **Overcrowding**

Signs of Health:

1) **Life-Related Bible Teaching**

2) **Effective Leadership**

3) **Believing Prayer**

A2.1.1a Steps To Influence

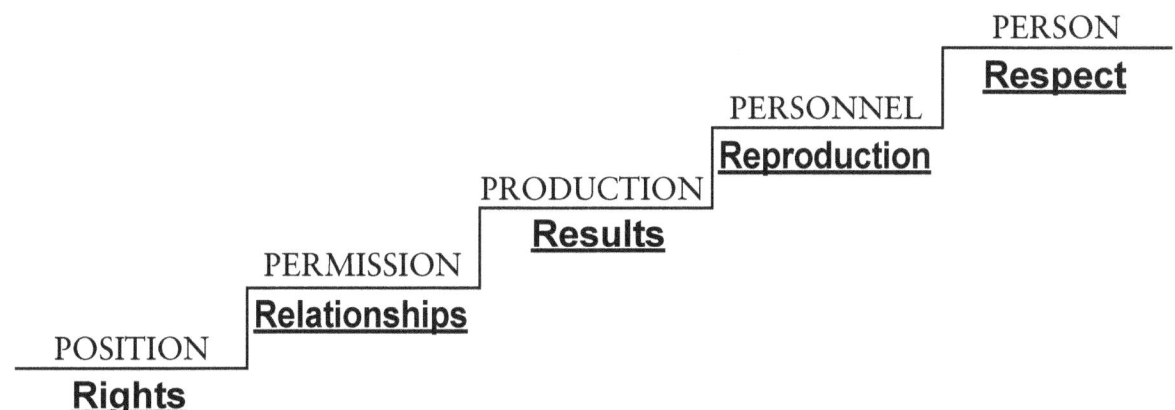

Step 1. People follow you because **they have to.**

Step 2. People follow you because **they want to.**

Step 3. People follow you because **of what you have done for the organization.**

Step 4. People follow you because **of what you have done for them.**

Step 5. People follow you because **of who you are and what you represent.**

APPENDIX 1

A2.1.1b Steps To Influence Insights

1) The higher the steps the **higher the commitment**.

2) The higher the steps the **longer it takes to get there**.

3) The higher the steps the **lower % of people who will follow you.**

4) The higher the steps the **greater the growth.**

5) The higher the steps the **more influence you have.**

A2.1.3a A Clearly Focused Vision

A growing church has a detailed description of the preferred future condition.

Definition: A more specific picture of what your church must be in order to accomplish its purpose.

The benefits of a clear vision statement are:

1) It will give us **unity**.

2) It will keep our **priorities** in order.

3) It will build **responsibility** and **accountability**.

Examples:

> **Our Vision**
>
> Reaching the Lost.
>
> Equipping the Found.
>
> Aiming for Excellence.
>
> Leading Responsibly.

APPENDIX 1

A2.1.3b Syndromes That Limit Your Vision

A) Problem Solving Syndrome

   When more time is spent **solving problems** than leading.

B) Busy Enough Now Syndrome

   When your ability to lead is limited by a **full calendar**.

   "Are you doing things right . . . or doing the right things?"

C) No Vacancy Syndrome

   When you become so content with the **people** you have, you don't see the need to bring more in.

D) Nostalgia Syndrome

   When you spend more time remembering the **past** than you do preparing for the future.

E) The Lazarus Syndrome

   When you spend too much time and energy attempting to recover **inactive** members.

A2.1.3c Selling The Vision

A) Preparing

    1) **Biblical** Priorities

        a) The Great Commission

        b) The Great Commandment

    2) **Pastor's** Strengths

    3) **Congregation's** Gifts

    4) **Present** Opportunities

B) Presenting

    1) **Vision**

    2) **Goals**

APPENDIX 1

A2.1.4 Clearly Established Goals

A growing church has detailed targets that will accomplish its vision and purpose.

Definition: A specific target.

1) The goal should be **specific**.

2) The goal should be **measurable**.

3) The goal should be **achievable**.

4) The goal should be **relevant**.

5) The goal should be **time bound**.

ANSWER SHEETS

A2.1.5 A Clearly Effective Strategy

A growing church will use the most practical,

proven tools to accomplish its goals.

Definition: A detailed course of action that moves a church to achieving its goals.

1) A strategy should match the unique **style** of each congregation.

2) A strategy should match the **resources** of each congregation.

EXAMPLE

<u>GOAL</u>: To increase finances 20%

<u>STRATEGY</u>: One month of stewardship climaxing with God's Guarantee

---

APPENDIX 1

A2.2.1 Biblical Background

FOR VOLUNTEERS

(Acts 6:1-7)

Observations:

1 (vs. 1) **Increased members but not ministers caused problems.**

2 (vs. 2) **Priorities and pressures demand volunteerism.**

3 (vs. 3,4) **Volunteers should meet qualifications.**

4 (vs. 5) **Congregation approved and volunteers selected. Don't value position but value workers.**

5 (vs. 6) **Volunteers approved for service.**

6 (vs. 7) **Growth resulted.**

Conclusion: The more qualified volunteers who minister, the greater the growth of the church.

ANSWER SHEETS

A2.2.2 The Volunteer Principle

A growing church needs to mobilize its members to active service for Chris in accordance with their gifts.

$$\boxed{\text{STAFF}}$$

$$\boxed{\text{LEADERS}}$$

$$\boxed{\text{VOLUNTEERS}}$$

(STAFF)	1) Set the **vision.**
(STAFF)	2) Recruit and train **leaders.**
(LEADERS)	3) Recruit and train **volunteers.**
(VOLUNTEERS)	4) Perform the **ministry.**
(BOTH)	5) Establish **accountability.**

APPENDIX 1

A2.2.3 The Pareto Principle
80-20

To grow, a pastor must invest 80% of his time into the 20% who produce 80% of the work.

80% of the people produce **20%** of the results.

20% of the people produce **80%** of the results.

MAINTENANCE ORGANIZATION

PASTOR	Serves the **80%**.	VOLUNTEER
20%	Do **80%** of the work.	VOLUNTEER
80%	Do **20%** of the work.	VOLUNTEER

GROWING ORGANIZATION

PASTOR	Equips the **20%**, **80%** of the time. Serves the **80% only 20%** of the time.	MODELER
20%	Are equipped to lead the **80%**.	VOLUNTEER
80%	Do the ministry of the church.	VOLUNTEER

A2.3.1 The Evangelism Principle

A growing church must incorporate evangelism into every area of ministry programming.

Step 1 **Make Your List** — Develop a prospect list of potential new members.

Step 2 **Pray Your List** — Enlist members with the spiritual gift of intercessory prayer to pray for all visitors, prospects, and those who will be going to the homes of potential new members.

Step 3 **Work Your List** — Follow Up!
Follow Up!
Follow Up!

KEYS TO SUCCESS:

- Think like an unchurched person
- Design intentional evangelism into your programming
- Elevate the role of evangelism in your congregation

APPENDIX 1

A2.3.2 "Reaching the Unchurched in The 2000'S"

In order for the church to effectively evangelize America, we must understand it has to be a multigenerational approach.

Some important facts:

1) **Must consider generation**

2) **Must consider communication method**

3) **All want to be recognized**

4) **All want to be loved**

As these generations are reaching middle age, their interest in the church is increasing. Why?

1) **Marriage**

2) **Children**

3) **Spiritual Questions**

A2.3.3 Increasing Visitor Flow: Making Your List

| STEP 1 | Advertising **6%** |

| STEP 2 | Programming **8%** |

| STEP 3 | Inviting **86%** |

APPENDIX 1

A2.5.3 Ideas for Meaningful Worship

- What steps can I take to add celebration, hope, and "success" to my worship?

    1 – Add Celebration Segments

    2 – Lighting

    3 – Flow

- If we are 80% full, what is our plan to provide more space for growth?

    _____
    _____
    _____
    _____

- What steps can we take to offer a full music program?

    _____
    _____
    _____
    _____

ANSWER SHEETS

A2.6.1 The Finance Principle[4]

A growing church must have adequate financial resources to underwrite growth expenses.

KEY RATIO: **$1.00** out of every **$10.00** in total church budget should be designated for outreach (NOT missions!)

1) **Finances** come from leadership, people involved in ministry, and exciting ideas
Teaching by Scriptures, illustrations, and examples of giving.
"People will pay for whatever they value!"
Tithing is last to arrive. Find out!.
Tithing is the first to go when mad. Find out! 6 weeks.

2) Financial growth **follows** people growth.
Lordship settles tithing.
Number of people increases finances.

3) Raising the finances gives you the **influence** to determine how they will be allocated.
You build it, you increase influence in budget.

---
[4] John Maxwell, Injoy Ministries ***

APPENDIX 1

A2.7 PASTORAL CARE

The Pastor or Pastoral staff will never be **sufficient** to take care of the needs of the congregation.

There must be a system in place in case you **leave**.

There are a variety of opportunities to provide pastoral care:

1) **Pastors**

2) **Small Groups**

3) **Board & Leadership Team**

4) **Age Groups**

5) **Ministry Teams**

Just Remember:

You are not the **Messiah**!

So recruit and train **help**!

A2.8 DISCIPLESHIP

The Great Commission calls us to make **disciples**, not just **converts**.

If you will keep focused on growing **people** and not just growing a **church**; then you will see the natural byproduct that is larger than **church**.

DISCIPLESHIP INVOLVES:

1) **INFORMATION**

2) **PROCESS**

3) **PERSISTENCE**

4) **RELEASE**

It just takes **work**!

A2.9 FELLOWSHIP

Fellowship in the building of **common purpose**.

Fellowship is the intentional pursuit of **relationship**.

Fellowship is the passionate calling to **share**.

Fellowship is the directive for **personal growth**.

Fellowship is the responsibility of a **Christ follower** to **connect** with other believers.

A4.1a Discipline 1: Hiring Staff

If you are going to grow a church, you can't be a **lone ranger**.

You will have to have **help**.

Hiring staff members requires:

1) **Patience**

2) **Searching**

3) **Relationship**

4) **Maturity**

5) **Volume**

6) **Time**

Where can you find good staff members?

1) In your **congregation**

2) **People** you've developed.

3) **Search organization**

4) Other **pastors/churches**

5) **Universities/colleges**

Two keys for finding and developing good staff:

1) **Patience**

2) **Persistence**

APPENDIX 1

A4.1b Discipline 1 (Cont.): Hiring Staff

THE FOUR C'S OF HIRING GREAT STAFF:

1) **Character** – Are they godly and are they good?

2) **Competency** – Do they meet the job requirements and can they do the job?

3) **Chemistry** – Can they work with others?

4) **Culture** – Do they fit the environment and atmosphere of your church and office?

A4.1c Discipline 2: Conflict Management

Conflict in a church or business is **inevitable**.

Everyone is **different** in how they handle conflict and how they **respond** to conflict.

   a) **Personality**

   b) **Pressure**

Knowing your **situation** is **imperative**.

Get the **facts** together.

Based on the different **personality types** involved determines how you **approach** the particular situation.

Delay will only cause more and maybe bigger **problems**.

Go into the conflict with **courage** and **compassion**.

Love them the next time you **see** them.

Don't **avoid** people in conflict in the **future**.

Don't make it **personal** even though it can be.

APPENDIX 2

ACTIVITIES

APPENDIX 2

CHURCH PICNIC

Go to a local park. Organize leadership with groups in charge of physical arrangements (tables, chairs, etc.), food (get men to grill hot dogs and hamburgers and supply chef hates), and entertainment (games, special music, etc.). Use name tags, dress casually, and end with Sunday Evening Vespers to replace church service.

FIVE, TEN, AND TWENTY YEARS ANNIVERSARY CELEBRATIONS

Invite former pastors. Recognize members who have been members longest and shortest number of years. Recognize all new members from last year. Use special music, preaching, and food. Use pictures and memories from past years.

INDEPENDENCE SUNDAY

Celebrate Christian citizenship on Sunday before July 4th. Use parade of flags and Pledge of Allegiance. Have children write about being an American. Decorate in red, white, and blue. Invite uniformed servicemen to follow flag parade. Use "God Bless America."

THANKSGIVING

Sponsor a barbecue and hayride on a farm, park, or at a church with clowns, helium balloons, old-fashioned games like bobbing for apples, sack races, pie-eating contests, etc. Conclude evening around a campfire with chorus singing and testimonies of God's blessings.

CHRISTMAS

Use live nativity, Christmas musical, and candlelight Christmas Eve service. Christmas caroling to hospitals and shut-ins. "Hanging of the Green"—when church family comes on one days and hangs all the Christmas decorations. Each family brings one ornament for the Christmas tree. Provide lunch afterwards.

EASTER

Palm Sunday emphasis with artificial palms given to each attender. Holy Week Services. Monday and Thursday–communion, Good Friday–resurrection, Easter Sunday–resurrection. Use music, drama, and lots of color and decoration on Easter Sunday.

ICE CREAM SOCIAL

Sunday evening, invite all visitors and anyone on your prospect list to a "Free Ice Cream Social." Advertise one month in advance. Serve cups of ice cream with toppings to make sundaes. Afterwards, have outdoor "Vespers" with upbeat, encouraging preaching.

SWEETHEART BANQUET

Around Valentine's Day, offer a banquet at a local restaurant, catered at the church or covered dish. Use individual tables instead of long rows. Candlelight. Special music. Decorate in red and white with lots of hearts and roses. Program options include the story of Ruth, Ephesians 5 (love wives as Christ loved the church), and testimonies about secrets of a happy marriage. End with recommitment of wedding vows.

CHURCH ANNIVERSARY

Celebrate your church's birthday annually. Invite city officials, members who have moved away, denominational representatives, and charter members. Display all pictures, old bulletins, dedication services, etc., that highlight the victories from your past. Saturday night and Sunday morning should include former pastors, leaders, etc. celebrating past victories.

FIND A PARADE

When your town or a nearby town sponsors a public parade, get an attractive banner, decorate a truck or a float, use a very warm slogan on the float such as "A Place for You" or "The People Who Care About People." Have children surrounding your float giving out individually wrapped pieces of candy to the spectators. <u>Raise</u> the image of your church in the eyes of the unchurched.

RENEWING YOUR VOWS

At the conclusion of a series on Marriage and Family or at the conclusion of the Sweetheart Banquet or on the Sunday preceding Valentine's Day, ask husbands and wives to stand, face each other, and repeat their wedding vows. Be sure to have them "kiss their bride." <u>Celebrate</u> marriage.

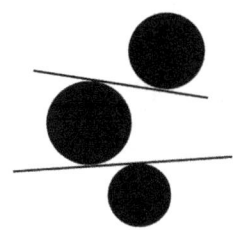

APPENDIX 3

CELEBRATIONS

APPENDIX 3

BAPTISMS

Perform baptisms at least once each quarter, preferably every two months and ideally every month. Announce weekly, one month in advance, the date and time of the next baptismal. Send attractive invitations to **all** relatives and friends of those being baptized. On the day of the baptismal, introduce the candidates to the congregation. Introduce the family and the persons who brought them to Christ and to the church. If possible, some candidates can give "two-minute testimonies." Sponsor a reception after church in honor of the new Christians/members.

COMMISSIONING MINISTERS

Publicly recognize every member of ministries and "commission" them. On Sunday morning, describe the vision of a ministry. Read the name of participants and bring them to the front of the sanctuary. Give each an **attractive** name tag identifying their ministry. Ask them to kneel and have official board or staff pray for them. They return to their seats as congregation applauds to show support.

MOTHER'S DAY

Advertise one month in advance. Special music. Recognize "oldest" mom and mom with the "youngest child present" and give sermon **centered** around godly mothers. Use one testimony in the morning. Have flowers or some other gifts to give to every mother present.

FATHER'S DAY

Same as Mother's Day except use men as testimonies. Great day for every child to bring their dad and recognize all dads with applause and prayer. Have a bacon bar or a burger bar for dads before and after service.

NEW MEMBERS

New members should be introduced to the church every month. Their picture should be on a bulletin board with their name and then they publicly receive a Membership Certificate. They should be joined by the person who first brought them to church. If they are involved in a small group and a ministry, announce them. After the worship, have entire church come to the front to welcome new members. Follow-up with a personal letter from the pastor telling them how pleased you are to be serving in this church family with them.

CERTIFICATE OF RECOGNITION

When a ministry group or an individual has done something that is very beneficial for your church, recognize them publicly with a "Certificate of Recognition." Do **not** recognize "position" leadership such as Deacons, etc. Always elevate people who are directly involved in ministry.

GRADUATIONS

Publicly celebrate graduations of High School Seniors, Vocational School, or College Students. Invite their families and friends to be present.Emphasize the family aspect of your church and how pleased your church family can be when a member graduates. Give a memorable gift to each graduate. Have a slide for each graduate recognizing high school, college, awards received, honors received, and future plans.

BABY DEDICATIONS

Send printed invitations to grandparents, parents, aunts, uncles, etc.Advertise one month in advance for participants.For parents who wish to dedicate their home as a Christian home.Give blue and pink Bibles as well as dedication booklets. Present letter to the mother to give to their child when they reach their 18th birthday. Example follows.

APPENDIX 3

Dear David,

I wanted to write you a letter and wish you a Happy 18th Birthday! I had the privilege of dedicating you to the Lord as a little baby boy on Sunday, March 19, 2005. You were the talk of the service that day. You stole the show as the people "oohed and awed" over you as I showed you off to the crowd. Your mom and friends were so proud of you that day.

You no doubt have grown up and I pray that you are serving the Lord with all your heart. There is nothing that would make your Mom as proud as she was on dedication day than if you are serving the Lord today! We gave you to the Lord that day and I pray you have given your life to Him. If you have not turned your life over to Jesus Christ yet it is as easy as ABC...

1) Admit you are a sinner

2) Believe in your heart that Jesus died and God raised Him from the dead

3) Confess Jesus as Lord of your life.

It truly is that simple! God has a wonderful plan for your life as you surrender to Him.

I hope you know that I love you as your pastor that dedicated you and if you ever need me please let me know. God has a wonderful plan for your life and don't settle for anything less than God's best. You will always be a special young man in my heart because I had the privilege of dedicating you back to Him.

Sincerely,
Pastor Dave
270.421.0898
Dave.deerman@gmail.com

www.ingramcontent.com/pod-product-compliance
Lightning Source LLC
Chambersburg PA
CBHW080913170426
43201CB00017B/2308